I AM TH

By the same author:

Dew and Broken Glass (2017)

As editor:

Arelhekenhe Angkentye: Women's Talk—Poems of Lyapirtneme from Arrernte Women in Central Australia (2020)

I AM THE GLASS

PENNY DRYSDALE

RECENT
WORK
PRESS

I am the glass
Recent Work Press
Canberra, Australia

ISBN: 9780645009026 (paperback)

A catalogue record for this book is available from the National Library of Australia

Cover image: 'Sea Eagle Nest' by Robyn Frances © 2020, reproduced with permission
Internal images: by Robyn Frances © 2020, reproduced with permission
Cover design: Recent Work Press
Set by Recent Work Press

recentworkpress.com

SS

for Lorraine and Eliza

Contents

I am the mild and obedient nurse
to this worn-out love.
I care for it, cradle it,
hold my temper;
I satisfy its few needs,
make good dinners, go to bed;
then all of a sudden
I say to myself: "What if I killed her?"

Patrizia Cavalli

One of the horses walks toward me.
His blue nose noses me lightly. I put my arm
over his blue mane, not holding on, just
commingling.
He allows me my pleasure.

Mary Oliver

1

you are a full stop or all these tiny dark endings

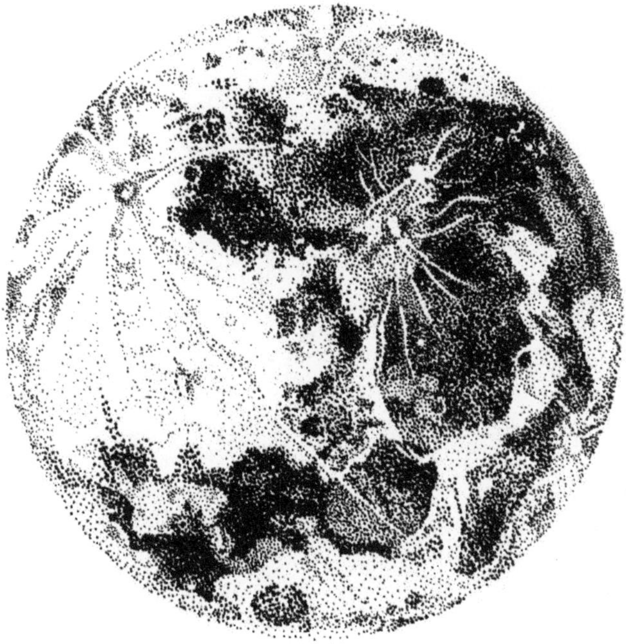

foam

light fluent kissing
of skin as each sphere ends
against you

I am the glass

you the sun

you dream you are drinking
from a fine stemless glass
you upend it with both hands
gulp down the contents
but you are anxious
scared of breaking it
the only one of the set
that is left my favourite
small enough for me
to grasp

she the moon

she gives us four new
champagne glasses
surprising
she rarely buys anything new
they ting together so sweetly
and she knows I love that
sound
the card reads
as each glass breaks over time
remember the joys
shared

her the sparkle

a bottle of champagne
on kitchen table
two glasses between us

we have survived a week
the week you went
to melbourne to see
if your fascination was real
you told me
you said goodbye to her
then you kissed and now
you can't help
that wide smile
as if by mentioning her name
I have given you a gift
she is there in the bubbles
between us

I the glass

I am the glass
with all this inside
my transparent walls
            the sun
            the moon
            the bubbles
            all this intoxication
I might tip
you out
before you get careless
and break me
we go flowing
across the floor
only me in pieces

pushing out

we assume that breathing in
comes first is the most important part
of this enterprise

but breathing out
is what matters

try to suck in more air
on each inward breath

go on! try it!

yes you can but this only gets you
so far

if you really want more air
in your lungs you have to push out
every last bit
a bit more than is comfortable
push it out all out
keep pushing it out

body heaves air back in
fills the void
you have left

man in the moon

after Rilke

the man in the moon
is not yet a man
or a woman
but a foetus

strange curled-up being
large head and torso
legs that have atrophied
and curled in confinement
little fists closed
in its sac of amniotic
mood fluid

I suppose it is waiting
to be pushed out

but instead it will shrink
into a crescent a nail a
hairline crack
then vanish

we look up each night
watching the gestation
again and again

how to get
this dark mass
outside us?

wet night alice springs

sitting under the back porch
dog crunching an old bone
at least she has left my thongs alone
still lying there under my chair
roughly in the shape of a pair
rain falling all around
after months without wet air
mist settling on my bare shoulders
it is a touch I have missed
behind me a house full
the light pushing outwards in squares
dish belled against dish
the sound of television
a one-sided conversation
a fraction too loud
she wants to watch the news
she wants to see what is going on
in the world
I want to see
the backyard wide-eyed
again glistening with water
I want to feel damp
mournful
to grow cold slowly
the natural way
without machines

to see that grey sky slide
into black
to lose confidence in outlines
to be still alone
to trust
this wet night

fallen

i.

out here we say what? to each other
more than any other
word

sorry-I-didn't-hear-you is
too much to repeat
every
time

rubbing each other's nose
in some deficit
when we are already
spent

one of us
back turned
walking ahead walking away
talking from the next room

one making sound so barely

fans droning on
above us and ahead
they relentlessly
turn

we wonder if it's the desert
or the years

ii

there's an old cactus in our
driveway

he's been there a long time
longer than you and I
he is over four metres tall with
a hundred arms
sprawling up
from a centre
shared

some single some
forked

each arm ending abruptly without a hand
on the end

each arm ribbed with pores
and at each pore a crown
of spikes lie open
brutal

among the spikes
green spears grow like
thick asparagus
clenched
shut
in the
heat

waiting for conditions to
improve

iii

yesterday a third of him
came crashing
down

in our driveway
our entry our
exit

our vehicles
parked in the street until
we work out what to do
with a thing
of this
size

the severed arms still crisp inside
with woody flesh of white
that soon will brown and grey and
rot

the spikes remain

we cannot wrap our arms around
his fallen arms
to drag him
clear

we stand and watch
his demise

all those tight spears
wasted

iv

you may think it not
much of a loss

but in the cool
of dawn those throngs
of spears remaining
will unfold
into a tissue-white flower
plush as a water lily
a broad face humming
with bees in the half
dark

bees nuzzling into inner yellow
threads

the pleasure won't
last long

the flowers
close and wither
dangle like
a blackened match
held too long
over a
candle

all these tiny dark
endings

angels as pests

you think every disturbance is beast | irritation | alien | something not supposed to be there at all | a fly | you bat it away | more come | a mosquito | you slap it on your leg | look distastefully at the streak of blood left upon your skin | you get repellent | apply it all over | this is how much control you want over your life | your body | your environment | you treat your angels as pests

what if you let them in? | notice out of the corner of your eye | give attention tend a wing | give some room to flutter wildly | of course they surprise you | as no doubt you surprise them | of course they are unfamiliar | other | as you are to them

but what sweet kisses they give | how sharp they bite | how they swell your body | your mind

what do they have?

every day I feed you
I put food in your bowl
though you've been out all night

though I've been up all night
I swear I will let you starve
but still I put food in your bowl

I wash all your things
hands drowning in water
up to my elbows

I should feel happy
I am capable
of such love

the ones who heal quickly
who move on
what do they have?

reaching

you don't often see a photo
of your own naked body
stretching towards someone
who is fully clothed who is
about to walk out of the room
walk through the streets
catch a train away from you
your arms flung around her neck
your faces pressing in one long kiss
not wanting to let go
the diagonal slope of your ribs
reaching up the arc of your
belly the curve of your white
skin against her black clothes the
sharp definition between you
until the place where your soft
darkness blends into black
clothes her bag on the bed
in front of you all zipped up
her arms wrapped around you
the wound on your elbow where
you fell her ponytail clasped
up high you sit here now recalling
her letting loose all that hair falling free
and being tied up again and falling free
the rubber band around her
wrist it being tied up again
and as hard as it is when that hair
is constrained you want to be
part of her rhythm all this
beauty and loss this freedom
and constraint this winding yourself
into a new shape who could see it
so clearly except through the eyes

of the other behind a camera
and how thin and hungry
you've become how careless
of your wounds how far
you are prepared to stretch
to be in her arms in this moment
before you part you are plant
winding towards sunshine
it is not possible I suppose
to grow any other way

greenhouse

I am sitting in my car in my own driveway | I am not getting out | I am not driving off | I am sitting here in limbo | It is cold outside | even colder in the house | but sunshine is trapped in this car | a greenhouse | and me growing inside it

sassafras

the flowers here are caged
but they don't have to be
sure the pademelons
might eat them
leaving sticks bare and broken
craving something to hold
something to show for themselves

sure the flowers might be digested
by furry hopping
creatures with delicate hands
with pouches for new life
who certainly will poo
on the soft green grass
they have worked so hard to keep short

new things will grow from that beauty
you were trying to save flowers
and leaves a little wilder in shape
even sassafras the tree so tall
and conical its leaves gently scalloped
crush them that smell it finds every
passage dissolves every blockage

coming apart

a tree loses bark after bark or a branch
with a crack

each leaf curls on the ground
and slowly browns

mulch around trunk once high and alive now
must accept whatever crawls through it

the waves push to reach shore
then withdraw

we try to hold onto everything we have
but our hair loses colour

there is one lash loose
upon a cheek if you ever come that close

and sometimes our toes or lower limbs
blacken and are taken

the air inside our lungs is lost to breath
but if we hold it we will splutter

that cloud will smother the sun
and then have to relinquish the rain

every drop will be lost
in the ocean what right do I have to hold on

to anything even frangipanis drop and rot
like tea-stained white cloth

and that boy on his scooter
one foot pushing

will lose his childhood
and his dad

koalas

we are the only koalas that can be seen
amongst fingers of long leaves eucalypts
hanging down she is wearing that flannelette
shirt the one she wore till we could see
right though it she is not looking
at the camera her eyes are closed as she laps
up this new love her smile so wide there is
a bulge in each cheek and that is where
the light sits I am sitting behind her
on the railing looking straight at the camera
its timer turned on our cheeks pressed and
for once we seem the same height my right hand
over her shoulder four fingers inside
her shirt just above the top button
my left hand under her other arm tugging
at the bottom button
                                                as if I am undoing her
for the camera

shell creature

your eyes are now closed but they move
beneath lids you squeeze and release
sometimes your eyebrows furrow
one tiny muscle in your cheek twitches
you look like you are going to cry and when

the artist pauses you always swallow
someone is holding your hand
with both hands one below as a platform
and one encasing your hand like the shell
of a snail and I photograph

this new creature your hands
this birth that has become our new death
the artist is making a pattern on your
belly the outline of a horse a raised hoof
a loose mane as it gallops through the interior

of a feather white highlights to bring
the image to life I can see your pain
is no longer my pain you have one hand
behind your head and with the other
you never let go of her hand

but the artist now needs to change sides
your new shell is broken for a moment and
you open and close your fist a few times
straining your fingers an invitation to me
to take up your hand as if it were now my turn

but my body steps back beyond reach
outside I photograph you both beaming
the light catching each patch of glad wrap
I see at last why she wanted me to come
and later when you leave me and I open

your mail which still comes to our box
I see she has made my photograph—shell
creature—into a card for your birthday
your thumb still poking through
the soft duct of her hand

doubt

i

when I doubt myself
I doubt you

ii

how could you love someone
so tired worn lame
the list goes on
worse still self-absorbed
all these imperfections
in my pool each rough edge
a shark the jagged teeth
the panic this trying
to swim away

iii

you are on the edge
naked beautiful watching me
the curve of your belly round
so much born from that place
I see in an instant
how foolish I look
swimming away from myself
the impossibility
if you continue
to love me now you too
are unworthy
of love

iv

yet I continue to hope
that you will dive in
with me and my sharks
you will peel off this last layer
of wet clothes let them sink
wrap your arms right around
and from this drowning
save me

v

oh I know it is only my own
confident stroke one after
the other—not in a pool
in the ocean—that will save me
that in the end I can't outswim
these sharks I must
swim beside them
knowing they maul and maim
knowing death will come
sooner or later it is this fear
I must turn to
learn to
love

without any words

I am held by a small strand
of casuarinas loose arms
reaching towards me

they whisper their sounds
without any words
I find it hard to walk away

so I stroke a low branch
a bundle of soft needles
as though it were animal

as though I were laying on my back
as though it were hair
hanging above me

nightcliff

it's sunday and I'm laid out on stone head propped up
looking at water I cannot enter
I have been dozing
a few strands of casuarina have fallen on my stomach
I leave them rising and falling
the ants are too busy
to bite it is the barely visible crabs who face the long haul
dragging someone else's carapace to cross rock
after rock
that is white or mustard or dry blood red the colour of a wound
just starting to heal over
birds land a black outline
framing egg blue faces a ship out there strange it still doesn't
seem to be going anywhere
just an artifice trapped between
two shades of blue trapped beneath voluminous white clusters
of bodies mostly women who lost
their heads or a limb waiting
for the next storm waiting to turn grey or turn dark or to make
an impact or perhaps to turn back
the birds make their noise
and it makes me remember where they came from just how long
it took to get here all of us to get here
only to leave and leave
again

see-saw

stand in the middle | gentle pressure | first
one leg | then the other | orchestrate your
movement | alone | you can | balance | it's your
weight | you can shift

plonk yourself down | on one end | look up at
the other | end empty | stuck high in the sky | by
your mass | at the bottom | your mind knows |
you can't move | at all | like this | and you
long | oh you long | to be up

someone to play | she circles the see-saw | do
you invite her | allow her | an end? | do you
squeal as you go up | howl as you go down | do
you bemoan | do you boss | do you try | to
control | but at least you are moving | what if |
she gets off | how hard will you hit | the ground
| what will break | was it worth it | that
view | from the top | the rise through the air |
you lean back to come down | your feet touch
the ground | straight up | and back down | the
momentum | the weight | of the other

experiment

what we need to do is
take off all our clothes
pin open our arms and legs
take a sterile scalpel
run it down our middles
look around inside
what is swollen
what is missing
make a map
with numbers and labels
repair what is vital
remove what is not
it is hard to do this
alone that's why
they make us
pair up

near the edges

a room filled with light
and all around us
wallpaper children
play in yellow and apricot
and milk brown

one is holding a kite
its tail like knotted stockings
nearby rabbits and puppies
wish they too could fly

two is kneeling and stroking
the chest of a lamb
as if in prayer

three is straddling a wooden fence
plaits parted as she climbs
to reach the last
dangling pear
for her basket

four is pushing a wheelbarrow
with a cat perched upon kindling

five has her knees drawn up tight
admiring a spindle of flowers
she has picked

and there is six with her hat pulled down
her hands holding the ropes as she swings
birds hover hair flies
but she has no face to carry her delight

there are butterflies here
but no snakes or rocks
or spiders or scabbed knees
no wolves or burning tigers
all the legs and arms of the children
are still attached

just near the edges the paper
has torn a piece flapping and a stain
seeping down from the corner
where a possum once died
in the roof

there are no reds or greens purples
blacks or blues
just toffees and honeys and fawns
leaping across our cursive
bodies in tender light a morning

after darkness in which we were
empty and hungry
pressing mounds into hollows
a long writhing puzzle
to see whether
we might still
fit together

clean sheets

I am grateful for clean cotton sheets
gentle green
though I was grateful for the grey linen
dirty ones too
my smell embedded in the weave
as I pull
the covers up over my mouth
and nose

seems strange to enjoy your own smell
on the sheets
some essence that the day dragged out of you
squeezed from your flesh
by some invisible pressure or harry
but delicious and necessary
there is no one else here
to inhale

I look in the mirror
these mornings
my hair trolled my eyes roiled
but I am glad for each sheet
for the clean and the dirty
the smell a small cue that each week
we must strip our beds
and start again

carried away

my fingers will find
every poem
written on you or in you
even the words hiding
beneath your hair
even the words invisible
in the folds of your skin
even the words coating
your teeth
and the ones you keep
pressed to the roof
of your mouth

I will trace each poem
on your belly
the small of your back
especially this forearm
that way you can read
one aloud to yourself
and hear it anew
perhaps you will feel
vulnerable and stronger
all at the same time

and without thinking
one thought you will throw
yourself open
the wings around you
will pause on your poems
as if they are wounds
or scars or flowers oh how
light you will feel
as you are carried away

you pilot you

you pilot you
you want me to be a passenger in your plane
to go wherever you fly
it will be an adventure you shout
   over your shoulder

well I want you to be
a beautiful meandering string of words in my new poem
but you are prose non-fiction ruled pages
I could tear off your edges but
you have already folded the corners down neatly
   they would tear in a straight line

you are a full stop.   but after a full stop there is always
   a little space

then a new sentence
   begins

darwin (a prelude)

I

today I bought yellow cushions to slash
my grey linen sheets / I wore a skirt
with red trees growing out of the darkness
branches set fire by the sun / I felt new
delight at the way each word
conjures another and another / you can
follow as they twist or turn / what they
tell / go to page 4 / page 9 / page 12 / you can
get past the haunted painting / a ghost
with gritted teeth tying you to an old
old story / yes you can / open
the big box not the small one / you can
you can / choose your own / ending

II

I did think I was clever coming here in may /
many suns going down / the cool off the water
festival after festival but then / the afternoons
grew into a womb and I became something
about to be born / a round thing made of
fluid lying in more fluid / a body without
edges / an inside seeping out / an outside
soaking in / a story with no beginning or
ending or words or form / instead of bearing
or breathing / the louvres I close / please
something electric / stop / my dissolution

III

on top of cliffs there is wind that thrashes
my faces / I lean out into it / the water
comes towards me / pulls away / I suppose
a human should expect this / my heart
is the sun sinking now / but this morning
it rose / and there is somehow a courage
to cross the sky / to give the world some new
colour and heat and a storm / and now
you tighten into a red ball / a glow / and you
sink into the ocean / I have to expect this
/ this burning / this dying / this promise / the
tender colour of your birth / or your death
the pang of your loss / that will come /
and the risk that / nothing will rise

bolt

you are working your way out
of my body I take off my shirt
to watch the weep of the wound
I decide to unscrew your ball
place you there on the table
beside three small red flowers
I photograph you in light
like a shrine on the grain
someone knocks on the door
I reach for my shirt scoop you up
in a tissue a secret in a pocket
it is gary in a t-shirt buddhist
orange he tells me he's grieving
he still wakes in the mornings
and looks around for the dog
he just buried I make tea in a pot
we sit out in sun and we hug
our own cups with cold fingers I can
feel you even now you are gone

driving out

it is hard to drive out
of desert in the rain

in your absence
everything will begin

to bloom

2

there were binaries to pack up or it looked
like a star had exploded

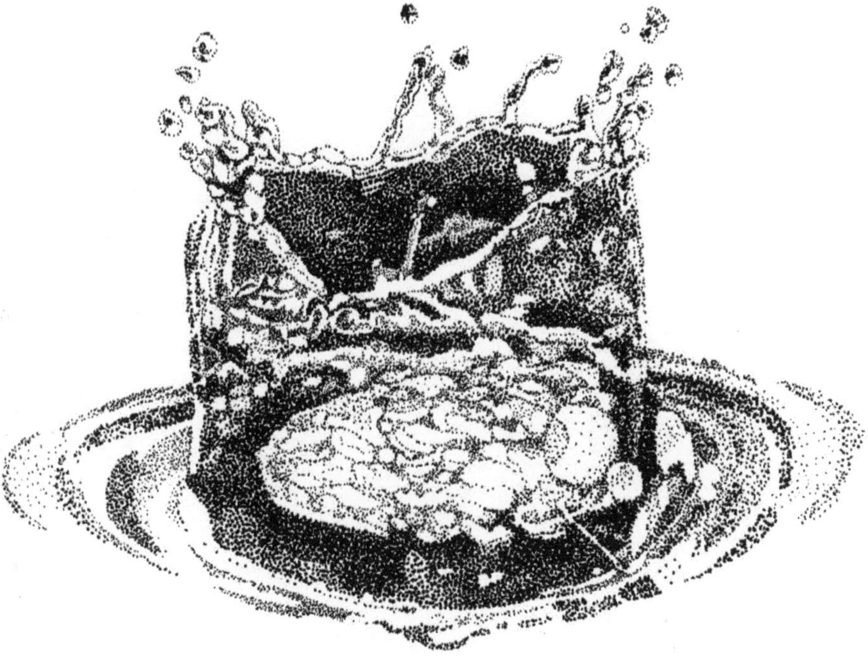

house at kennett river

it was the first time the first place
we spent a weekend
  away

we got to know it then we didn't leave
although outside the ocean was
  swelling

we took the clock off the wall we couldn't
stand it ticking wanted nothing
  from outside

the glass box in the corner held fire
and we were drawn
  inside

later there on the stair I braced myself against you
held the banister watching water run down
  the windows

and remember at the top of the stair
that crazy painting it is
  still there

a woman playing feet bare wild horizontal hair
her keyboard rolling away from her
  like a wave

now four years later I am here alone
pushing around coals
  in this fire

I am here to put my self at last
into this piece
  of work

I confess

that night in the car I confess
I love wind moon and night
more than you

we had been out to a restaurant
for dinner we left early
I didn't want to go home
we drove out undoolya rd
past where the bitumen ends
past where the phone signal ends
I pushed the buttons
that opened the windows

we were new and we didn't
even know where the hill was then

there was a breeze from the desert
from somewhere out there
a bit cooler than skin
I kicked off my shoes
hitched up my skirt
I poked my bare legs out
the window lay back
the caress of that breeze
across skin that was mine
that wind saw me and knew me
it followed my curves
in a way that felt rare

I lay there not talking
while the wind touched my skin
until you got bored and said
you wanted to go

microscope

I held you in the swimming pool
this morning because I thought
you were going to cry again
the sun scattered circles of light
on your shoulders all wet and salty
        and as I squeezed you tighter
        loosened my hold
        and squeezed again
they collided or drifted apart
like cells under a microscope
a thousand moments of conception
and near misses and I wondered
what opposites inside you
were struggling to unite
what new life on the verge
        of being born

pierced

ω

I didn't want a bolt
I fantasised about a gold ring
small and delicate I didn't realise
they have to measure you up for size
the nipple I mean and for the first three months
you are required to wear a titanium bar
a round knob on each end to hold it in place
like a barbell for an insect metal grey
it's not even that attractive but jesse said
you need something perfectly straight
to prevent infection and when my ears were done
forty years ago I had a straight bar too
in those days it was shot in with a gun
jesse advised they didn't use guns in his studio
it causes damage to the tissue
I couldn't even have gold
titanium is the most inert metal recommended
to prevent a reaction a rejection
the bolt was thicker than I imagined
to prevent tearing jesse said

ω

there is something onomatopoeic
about the word 'piercing'
say it out loud 'p i e r c i n g'
the 'c' makes a long 's' sound
when it follows the 'ear' sound it seems to extend the word
unnaturally like a sharp instrument pushing through flesh
even the closing of lips the force of air
required to make the 'peh' sound
reminds me of that first push in

ω

you couldn't know what I was like before
I think the most accurate word is 'impermeable'
I was inside a house and everyone was outside or I was
outside and everyone was in always these walls
and a strange sense I didn't belong
where everyone else was
I was lonely and I craved someone to open me up
but I didn't know how to go about it
I had fantasies of course
someone more powerful than me
but I could never act them out
in the beginning my partner tried to make
some kind of opening
it worked while our love was fresh
but I became good at resisting her I had to be
I suppose in the end she gave up trying
humans were never intended
to have that much control
the universe is meant to flow
in and out of us
like breath and words
all kinds of liquid
and moonlight

ω

it grew on me or in me
or I grew around it at first I didn't dare touch
I was a strict adherent to jesse's rules even
where my own hands were concerned
the bolt made my nipple harder and more prominent
than the right one which seemed flat and lifeless
barely distinguishable from the skin around it
but the left one well it stood for something
and I started to find it beautiful and erotic

it seemed more prominent whether I touched it or not
and when I squeezed with my finger and thumb
the bolt seemed to be doing its own pushing from the inside
as if the bolt had a touch independent of my own hand
it's the definition I like a hard bold departure
from the soft skin all around
it makes me want
to arch my back the way she did
and dare to ask
for something
I haven't yet received

honey

I had never seen
her cherish food
the way she did that honey
holding the unlabelled jar
in both hands
admiring the colour holding it up
to the window
so she could watch it glow
gold turning it tilting it
watching the thick liquid roll
she kept slowly repeating the line
there is honey
and there is honey
as if it were a new truth
she had never heard before

I stood at the end of the bench
looking into my cup
watching the tea turn black

more honey

she brought more honey
on the plane from sydney
and the lid came loose in her bag
that would ruin my weekend
I thought
but she seemed delighted
as if this proved
how utterly uncontainable
her honey was

honey and broken glass

from the bedroom I heard her
cry out and I thought
she has sliced off her hand!

but when I arrived in the kitchen
she stood still
over smashed glass and honey
which had already settled
in its new shape on the floor

it looked like a star had exploded
a hemisphere left at the impact
stellar shards and triangles radiating out
getting larger the further
from the centre they lie

she was not mopping it up
she was photographing it

this kind of disruption
a new gift to be shared

recipe

we cooked dinner together most nights | we always had a glass of wine although sometimes she would have a beer and I would have a g&t | we tried to get dinner ready in time to watch the 7 o'clock news | I always took charge of the vegetables cut everything up laid them out on the chopping boards | she always cooked the meat | this was how our evening proceeded after busy days at work | it was friendly full of camaraderie | we talked and debriefed as we prepared the food | a loving look a hug kind words to soothe whatever hurts the day brought | there were not usually complicated recipes to follow | we mostly cooked the same limited repertoire of dishes | if we had white wine she always had ice and I never did | we knew how it was going to roll | we didn't have to negotiate | we were quite proud of this when we heard other couples bickering in their kitchens | only occasionally would I have to remind her | she was easily distracted | about the timing of the meal | and soon it was 7pm and there were two reasonably healthy meals sitting on the coffee table | a top up of wine | pepper and salt | favourite condiments | and serviettes because she grew up with them

eggs

this morning I cooked eggs

isn't it strange how you always
cooked eggs so beautifully and I became
the one who broke
every yoke in the pan

I was only trusted
with the toast and the tea

even bacon belonged to you

Ω

I don't mean this was your doing or mine
you just cooked what you were comfortable with
and I cooked up my own comfort too

but we were somehow defined by each other
we knew our place in every binary

dark / light
interior / exterior
introvert / extrovert
pessimist / optimist
spiritual / physical
solitary / social
moon / sun

even now you know you are on the right
if I am on the left and the forward slash
can't be climbed

we did try different sides of the bed but if
we changed places more often maybe
something else could have hatched
and imprinted on new mothers

with someone new I know / you could be
someone different

but with me / could you
ever be?

Ω

in our messy demise I recall
you wrote poems on a swing and descended
you lived and you travelled alone
while I ran and I talked and I moved I got better
at sharing and risking without hiding or blaming

I thought this was a small hope
I could push the word 'us' out of my new womb
you might catch it with new hands

though perhaps our love only lived and was lost
to change us
it finished the job so it quit

Ω

but my eggs this morning
were perfect without me even thinking
about how

the yokes didn't break till I was seated
at my table

and my knife entered gently
at just the right angle
and the yellow spread from its sphere like
it really wanted me
and I wanted it

just the right pepper the salt and the heat
in the chutney

every last morsel of toast tasted
opulent yellow

Ω

I ate outside in the garden
that you've never seen
its giant hand-like leaves and its lace
each arch waving a bit more wildly
tendrils falling carelessly and yet it appears
well-curated

the dragonflies have red bodies that throb
which today I can see because they land
so close to me and they stay
just long enough

the dry season has arrived star fruits
hang off trunks with each clutch slowly
ripening

there are berries and cheese fruit
and bright pink flowers that return
every day although once
they poisoned the cat

Ω

that frame you gave me I never liked much
is in the garden too
greying and becoming part of everything else
it has no photo or glass
creatures and light just dapple right through
the place where we
sat side by side
in that roofless russian jeep
by the river in prague
your hands on the wheel
pretending to accelerate
not yet knowing we were going nowhere
me throwing back my head
laughing was I envying?
your relentless bravado

Ω

what frames allow their interiors
to change

must we set an image behind glass
in the effort to stop it entering
its great deterioration

is an open frame better to weather
the crawl of creatures
and the flowering of mould

I am trying to get better at taking out
each square of glass
without such shatter
or smash

Ω

I know it won't be long
another great upheaval
there always is

till then I am climbing every forward
slash and allowing myself to fall
over the edge

there have been many uncomfortable
landings

but today I am happy to crack and to cook
my own eggs and to lick that last crust
of yellow

to sit in a garden where yellow falls
from the sky
and lands on an outside that once
was within

portrait

she has drawn me in blue texta on a page overlaid
with some kind of grid a cage that runs right
through me

I am shaped like an egg a tuft of hair of course stick
arms jutting out where my ears ordinarily are

I have two legs though one is badly broken in two
places there is a nasty bifurcation below the knee
hard to stand on my feet like this but my feet
have been forgotten

my mouth is crooked and turned down
puckered in this confusion to stop unnecessary
items getting in or out a tiny nose the shape
of a heart or a bee a little small a little lost
its sting already spent

my eyes are isosceles not a disease but two
triangles turned upside down one vertical one
horizontal it has slipped and I accept they are not
so good for seeing anymore

on what she thought was the top the teacher
has written "This is Penny" in the same blue texta
and the words "Love from Eliza" beneath it

there I lie on my side looking sad and befuddled but
well-labelled my stick arm stretched out though no hand
to hold or be held

I have come off my wall I am the egg who has fallen
of course this is how she must see me

lying in wait

I lay alone—in a giant bed—every time
I breathed—the covers touched me—here—
and here—and here—there was a tenderness—a gentle pressure
I nuzzled in—I was the face of a horse pressing into the chest
of my owner—my hand rested in the hollow —
between hip bone—and belly—I felt my own
belly move my hand up and down—up and down
— as I breathed—the hand was not used to moving
without muscle—volition—it was used to being in charge —
to feeding that belly—to scratching it

I was there—in a warm safe place—for an unknown time
nine hours—nine minutes—nine months—no part of me wanted
to swing my legs out into cold—where everything
was edge—hands holding instruments —
metal tools—teeth—greetings

standing in wait

I watched it fall on grey tiles
run along the white grout
as though it were guttering

it dribbled down as if my legs
were the sides of a tin of paint
it kept falling—red rain

a strange absence of shame
a surrender a wonder without
any womb what more can be born?

but there were binaries to pack up
into pairs and a hotel room
like a womb to check out of

broken moon

moon broken moon
still in the daylight sky
you hung above me in the dark

the morning she drove away
while I sat in 5am sand and retched
shadows flew past without faces

as if abandoning the birds
and bats they belonged to
you watched me try to write

without light I couldn't find where
to put down the pen I couldn't make
one word follow the other

no doubt you followed her too
all the way to the airport
you have been up there now

every morning since
but soon you will stop
being broken you will be gone

fishpond

It may have been a fishpond, had it contained any water, or any fish. In the absence of those things, it was, of course, a hole in the ground.

I couldn't decide if it was the shape of a tear, or a womb. The bottom and sides had been smeared with concrete, now cracked in four or five places, the edge circled by rocks, concreted into position, softened by dry grass, intruding into its interior, tangled gold, waving over the barest of rubble.

At the narrower end, three large rocks had been set, as if edging a gorge, a castle with three towers, one taller than the other two.

In tan boots I stood on those rocks, one leg bent, like a farmer, or a soldier above a grave, my pen a gun resting in my hand, looking down on this absence of water,
this space inside me, without any fish.

anger as a knife

Ω

elders know names are important
use them with care

when I see her name flash on my phone
I flush with old tenderness

and I answer like that all opened up
to hurt yet again

so I change her name in my phone to kumanjai:
the one who has gone

a reminder each time to close in what is moist
before I pick up the phone

Ω

I spoke to my mother on the phone
and she told me that after dad left

every time a plane flew over the house
she thought it was him

looking down looking out
for us

Ω

it's another weekend and I'm not
getting on with my life

I am looking at my phone
for a message from her

and I really expect one until
I remember how long it has been

Ω

is it slicing me free
or is each little cut a connection?

is anger a knife or a fire
demanding of fuel?

days spent with an axe
chopping up wood

Ω

in tiny script in the centre
of the page I put down

I am angry because she doesn't
love me anymore

and I can't seem
to make her

on the next page I write
I am angry so angry

at myself
what I wasted

and the words grow bigger
more crazed as I scrawl

I press in so hard the page tears
and the imprint of words

can be read on the next page
and the next and I turn and I turn

and it takes a long time
for the pages beneath to be free

of anger pressed in
pen like a knife

the wet of her eye

I lay in bed arms around her
that face nuzzled into my chest
I drew little circles on her arm
as if that motion would bring
her back to me   I could feel
the wet of her eye soak through
cotton cold against my skin
the things that are good in this
world I said are so close
to the things that are bad

shower poem 2017

I remember sitting cross-legged
in the empty bath every day
massaging my hair with shampoo
and knowing no matter how hard
I press it will never feel as good
as someone else doing it
washing myself slowly with a hose
watching the water run down
seeing the shape of my body
the curve of my belly how tight
my legs were from running the dark
wild parts of me I remember opening
the folds of my skin the soft pink
the interior and washing the caress
of warm water the clearing away
of the lather washing the mounds
of my breasts holding and washing
beneath that foreign object
in one of my nipples I remember
shaving the hair off each leg and then
sitting on a cushion on the floor of
a room that wasn't mine rubbing oil
avocado into each leg till it glowed

shower poem 2018

when I pulled back the shower curtain
she looked wide-eyed startled as though
I had dragged her out of another world
with both hands she wiped the water
and her fringe up off her face then she held
out her hand took my hand in hers
                                                                she
squeezed shampoo into her palm and when
I went to do the same she said no
this is for you
                        she started to wash my hair
and I stood facing her crying with
the pleasure and the pain of what she was
doing she moved slowly and when she had
washed out the shampoo she did the same
with conditioner gently combing out the
tangles with her fingers water streaming
down my body an occasional animal
noise
        she held the soap and lifted each arm
and washed underneath and my torso my
breasts my back and my shoulders slowly
lathering the soap while I cried it was
orange and poppy seed a sharp citrus
smell and she rinsed it all off
                                                I started to
shave my legs leaning my foot on the bath
she didn't get out she kept on washing me
and I kept crying and that's how we were
when the water went cold
                                            she tried turning
the water off and on to kickstart the heat
but I knew the gas was all gone

shower poem 2020

I picked up a sponge and started
cleaning the shower a strange
gentle pressure on the glass
the tiles every little corner
where the mould had gathered
every edge and the shower
pushed back as it trusted
what I was doing at last
white bars wore clear
on the shower door a few
drips ran all the way down

I got a glimpse of myself
in the mirror each sweep
each curve an un-cumulation

I thought this is a really beautiful
shower and I kept washing
I didn't think I must hurry I have
oodles to do I didn't resent dirt
or discolouration or blame
the mould in patient curves I tended
one hand temple-pressed
against glass and the other
circling with sponge I took down
each bottle and wiped gently
the sides each little bottom
I scraped off a crust with my nail

I got out all loosened and I rubbed
my legs with soft cream
I breathed oranges and
mandarins what work they do
I saw the silver tap had started

to gleam and I smiled it is my
mother who made taps like that
how I thought she was wasting
her time and I wondered why

I spent all these years rushing
past taps I touched every day
mildly annoyed that I couldn't
control the brown circles
building where everything fitted
together

jumping up at me

I was driving through eastside
in a bus with no passengers /
out of the corner of my eye
I saw you little dog / my heart

leapt in the air / I had written
you a letter / but I didn't
have a clue where it might find you /
now you were pulling on a woman

who was pulling on your lead / I
parked up on the corner but by
then you were gone / I feared you
vanished behind a doorway or

a fence little dog and my one
chance to hold you was lost /
right down chewing street I chased you
calling out / like a mad thing / wait!

excuse me! / and she turned so did
you little dog / you looked a bit
puzzled / cocked your head to listen
intently / it had been a long

time / you remembered / came bounding
across the road little dog / not
looking just dragging your keeper
behind / you jumped up on me / bad

dog! / as you always did / rolling
on your back shaping your body
into a C / and I scratched and
I rubbed / your tummy quite roughly

just the way you like it / a big
smile on your face / and I noticed
we were lying right on the road
little dog / you lay like a C

as I stroked you little dog
lapping up the affection / I
explained to the woman / who was
izzie / that I was fran's partner

well ex-partner / do you mind if
I pat this little dog / as though
it wasn't too late to ask her /
but if I needed any proof

of who I was little dog / your
reaction was definitely
enough / and I pushed back the tears
as I spoke little dog / it seemed

izzie'd not known I existed /
you don't live in town anymore
she inquired / and I babbled
little bits about you / and I

asked if you'd been good little dog
knowing full well the answer / she
told me you bark quite a lot
and that's been the main problem since

fran has been gone / oh poor little
dog from a broken-up home
your barking was always a boon
for us / no one ever broke in

to our house little dog / and in
a while I thought it polite to
get up / and I stood / said goodbye /
walked away / and you little dog

departed with izzie / but you
kept twisting around / a mad thing /
to see where I was / and you pulled
on your lead back towards me /

as always I thought you would choke
so I ran back towards you / I
never was quite so happy and
sad all at once / and I called out

to izzie I'll have to walk you
both home / little dog never liked it
if her people were parted / she
did the same thing to fran and to me

if we ever were walking and
we needed to part / I raved on
to izzie of that old afternoon
the soccer grand final and right

after the match I tried to walk
you straight home / so fran could join with
her teammates for a drink / but you
dug in your heels / hunkered down low

you could not be moved little dog /
fran had to come with us back home
and once you were safely locked
inside the gate we went back to

the bar / and all this I babbled
at izzie as we walked / who may
not have been interested /
and we went up the path into

her house which had walls of deep green
like our place once did / and a girl
in the kitchen was standing at
the bench / you ran for your water

and I thought I should leave / but you
ran back to me / flopped onto your
back in the shape of a C / and
I gave you a massage right there

on the floor / while the breakfast was
cooked / I was determined to love
you / I wasn't ashamed / and I
offered some fragments of our past up

to izzie / tried to seem normal
so I didn't have to leave /
it was hard as I sat /
on the floor right beside you

repeating / I love you little
dog / I'm sorry little dog / so
sorry little dog / I didn't
explain much to izzie or the

girl in the kitchen exactly
why I was sorry / coz I knew
you already knew little dog /
I was sorry that I didn't

love you enough / all those years that
we had / and I knew that you knew /
and I knew you forgave me / this
lifelong failure to love

3

a stone amongst stones or how else
can a branch be?

spoon

there is sadness in honey
the way it clings
to the spoon

fork

let's dissolve the storylines one fist
full of salt into ocean

I could stay hungry and angry at you
or I could practice tonglen over and over
taking in your pain in exchange
for my loving kindness or ring you over
and over apologise for trying to bully you
into loving me apologise for punishing you
for not loving me for telling you again and again
you've made a mistake

but even that act
of contrition is holding on as I rehearse
the words letting go

in the distance a child is on this same
swing it goes back and forth and she squeals
with delight screams with distress

there are branches above me now
that fork and fork and keep on forking
till each tine is fettled by the repetition
by relentless separation how else
can a branch be?

weathered basket

how times have changed
when your greatest happiness
is to look
with satisfaction
at a pile of sticks gathered
in a weathered basket

or a stack of wood against a house
the logs once separate
settle in together an armless
holding being held
a rolling rhythm a rapport
pressed upon a wall

horse and swallow

galloping horse treads on the back
of a swallow flying

a hoof pushing off
a back

the horse's tail erect
head cocked to one side
nostrils flaring
mouth ajar half laugh
half scowl

he doesn't look down
to see what damage he's done
he races through sky
accelerating

all that bravado in one wired body

the bird prostrate beneath him
pushed into marble

a tiny living platform

the body of a tree

Lake Conjola

the body of a tree juts into a lake—oh light

is failing
water lapping
dark body
splayed in cold
the lower bough wears
a green slip a shroud
a body washed
as bodies are

spiders have woven soft cloth—between

sticks that stretch
away from each other
there is no point now
chasing day over hill
light is crowning

in some other country—light

is leeched from
ordinary objects
evening fuses everything
grave-blue-green the colour
of hardened rock
once lava hot
accelerating down

the side of a mountain—cresting

waves do try to push or pull
the body in the body
out the body immovable
a long time now
this wheedling of water

the body will rot I suppose till then—birds

have a platform
they are not here now
of course there
is no singing
except the wash
of water stroking
old jetties

hard now to find my footing—no reason

to move but darkness
the little steps I take
require standing
bats are active inside
my body the vibrations
help them see

a sheoak hangs a soft frame—for what

this lapping
this failing
of a surplus
I once called light

invisible journeys

I see a feather alone
on rock the wind
pushing her a little —

she is calling for a lightness
of touch a respect
for freedom
an acceptance that we lose
the very things
that once helped us fly

out jumps a wren
so blue it hurts
when I look at her
yet it hurts
when she is gone

the weaving of air
by birds
leaves no product
no prize no trace
there is no straw
turned into gold

yet the leaves say
shhhhh watch
these tender
invisible journeys

white feather

(LETting GO)

you were once attACHEd to a bird   did you like life then?   such light fluff
on the wing of a being   do you feel dead now that you are seveRED?
or was attachMEnt living tORture?   to be controlled by mUScle
by a brain SO Small   is it only now released   you dare to
quiver   move through air alONE   rest on ground
without   being folded   comPRESSed with
all tHEse copies of yOURself?   but I see
you are caught   on a bRANch
stILL not free eNOugh to float?
BIRD   that old leviathan
fLAPped you   away
from such   SHarp
barbs for FEAR
you'd sTICK
to soME
one
el
se

magpie geese

we've come in to land
we've come a long way
we are together for a while
then we have to go
but in this our season
we share low groans of love
and the relentless rearrangement
of ourselves

thirty million steps

found poem—the words of Marina Abramović

For eight years Ulay and I
had been requesting permission to
do
a
performance
piece
on the Great Wall
of China.
Our plan
was to
start
at opposite ends, walk toward each other,
and get married
when
we met.
By the time
the Chinese
finally said yes,
our relationship
was over.
I have never been one
to give up a good opportunity,
so
we
decided
to still walk
toward
each other
but say good-bye
instead

when we met.   It was extremely
painful. To make things worse,
I knew
at the time
that Ulay
had made
his Chinese guide
pregnant
and would
soon
be having
a child.

progress

there was a girl
in a magenta dress
with a white puppy
a black patch
over one eye
he was exuberant
so free of convention
he neither walked nor
paused to sniff or wee
he was on a lead
which he kept
biting and tugging
jumping up to be closer
to her wrapping
his front legs around
her legs it was hard
for her to walk like that
especially once
she picked up her latte
but progress didn't
seem to matter

song for a weary throat

after RAWCUS Ensemble, Theatre Works

I remember the darkness
a woman standing on a chair writing
across a blackboard in white chalk
at the midpoint of my life I found myself in a forest
so dark that my future
was blotted out

I remember the light on a sad face a hand reaching
towards a sky a couple dancing
three singers standing beside each other
no words at all no instruments
just a haunting sound coming towards us
the sound of loss ringing out

I remember the props and the people
constantly rearranging themselves I thought yes
of course that is what people do
rearrange themselves and their stuff especially
when faced with a crisis that's what
I have been doing

I remember all that activity everyday life
smashed by a single clap of light and sound
as if the loudest crack of thunder the brightest flash
of lightning were combined in a single shard
a shard not a shatter shattering
goes on for longer

pieces of broken glass fall somewhere and that falling
the hitting of floor makes sound and after light
and sound and fear there is darkness people running off the edge
of a ramp running over the edge   a great leap
some land and run on some fall each person
never knew what

would become of them and people crawling on stomachs up
the ramp to get higher people rearranging furniture to climb
higher and a single illuminated hand reaching higher
I remember a girl asking every person in the room
to dance and not one person said yes not one person
rose to their feet

not one person took her hand yet she kept asking all around
the room because that's what she wanted to dance with someone
all this loss and grief people knitting reading books holding each other
but for every person held there was a separation I remember
a light a dark a love a separation there can be
no other ending

no one deserves to die

no one deserves to die
on our roads the sign says
even here so I stop
in dystopia woven with an air
that is blown by conditioners
even here where the bricks are
not real where the signs tell you
what-not-to-do on each wall
where someone has sawn
branches once hanging their
welcome either side of the drive
where the stumps are still raw
the colour of sawdust
where there's a shortage of
nutrients to feed all the plants
they look starved in blue gravel
a road without tar to hold
things together where toyotas
have arches like eyebrows
drawn high above their wheels
even here there are palms
with no fronds and hedges
hacked into dicks that don't
match and a path edged with
bushes not one daisy left
cooked off in afternoon sun
even here there is bunting
to mark off a space that is
nothing but empty and each
plastic chair its companion an
ashtray and the failing light
falls on reception to soften
the no vacancy sign and
birds sit on limbs that are

severed and something gold
is dying over my shoulder
it still feels too hot to go inside
even here where the sweetness
is stifling and laced into curtain
and swimming up from carpet

driving south

three days at Port Germein
the longest wooden jetty in the Southern Hemisphere

i colour

the wood on the jetty is grey
and the railings are grey and the bolts
that hold the whole thing together are grey
the bench seat the sky and the water are grey
the hills in the distance are grey

I might be grey too but I am wearing
a pink skirt with red flowers
the wind keeps lifting it off my knee
and setting it back down it throws
hair across my face and it doesn't feel
like criticism it feels like someone saying
I will find you I will find you

lapping is soothing but also a teasing
there are curls that have calcified and
barnacles clinging to bridge
at the end there are pedestals with a black
and white bird posing on each one
it gives me confidence that grey can again
be divided into darkness and light
and a blush of peach from somewhere
may arrive

red starts to burn on the horizon
a sun can't resist its own setting

ii dissolution

the sound of lapping is soothing
this water with curls and scallops
and dollops of foam washes the wooden stairway
the concrete base it pushes at each solid thing
and I'm sure dissolves some of it
or at least dissolves its confidence
it was once was quite solid soon the sand
the concrete the stair with myself sitting on it
will be rolling away from the shore
out from under the jetty
and off towards some horizon

the water says come come I am an armful
of loose weed without muscle or will

iii questions

is this jetty or gang plank? I think
as I walk it is the longest in the world
when I get to the end there is no drop
into nothing but a row of weathered
pylons still adorned with the rusted
chains and bolts from a past
below the surface more barnacles are
soaking their worries in green water

the cormorants are resting heads hidden
or posing bold necks bent as if each
is a preposterous question on a pedestal
they vie for position one growling at another
voices like whispering chain saws
every pole every bird a different height
a different angle I wonder what
they are exalting or hunting as the darks
lurk closer to surface

tiny yellow marks like tears can be seen
in the corners of their eyes

iv horizon

they race across water
splashing and beating the surface
until they are clear

and in the calm one sleek black fin
rises and disappears
here over there the repetition
leaves me scanning for something
I don't know if it is dolphin
or shark or ray but it is here like a human
to bring up the fish

something else for me to find and lose
lose and find between here and horizon

elsie's house

I walk along the street
the dead tree by the driveway
two trunks stretching apart
barely a leaf between them

inside is empty the blinds are all open
a dark house but for a light at the back
I can see through the windows the hooks
where we once hung our hats

behind me a noise that is jarring
the neighbours are wheeling their couch
across the road and the grate of the wheels
fills the night as they cross

I stay in the shadows just watching
slowly moving down the street as disguise
I am wraith or ghost and I can't help but think
someone wanted me to witness this shift

I feel happy that a small girl called elsie
will live in this house her swing already up
elsie was my grandma's name too
and the name I had picked for a child

it will be elsie's house now her new
little home I am concerned for her welfare
I wonder what they will do
with the tree by the drive

two trunks stretched apart ugly and
leafless and lifeless hanging over
the swing still there all these years
no one with the courage to cut it down

passage into light

some mornings she leaves the house in near darkness
it is quiet enough to see a mouse running atop a fence
a spot in the sky grows raw pink and a great thumb

presses into the wound and smears it everywhere
she is certain someone laid these frangipanis down
so she could follow this path this scent merging

like this she is led towards the fullest moon it is setting
over water and she knows she will have to wait yes wait
she keeps walking and the breeze makes her skirt flap

she twirls a little corner round her finger like a lock of hair
she notices ocean shunting shore one white tongue always
more eager than the rest it almost sounds like applause

hurt locker

after Penny Byrne, Hurt Locker, blown glass, steel, 2015

What I notice about you first is a sound [] a heart
pumping [] although it is not [] in your body [] it is coming
[] from behind me [] somewhere else entirely.

I notice the steel cage from which you are made [] tiny squares
bracing each other [] your whole body [] a patchwork
of protective clothing [] shoes covered over [] as if you work []
in an operating theatre [] fireproof gloves [] for lifting something hot
[] not out of an oven [] your face completely protected [] dark
glasses [] a nose with two triangles [] wise I suspect [] noses
are often broken [] your jaw [] heavily reinforced [] my knight
[ ] in glass armour.

Your shoulders are broad [] not in the superman way [] in the way
of [] bathroom plumbing.

The other thing I notice is the light [] refracted in your squares seems
black [] from a distance [] but up close [] a strange deep pink
[] red [] glints of orange [] impossible to name [] this
colour [] I thought [] sometimes [] the colour [] of a newer
deeper [] bruise.

I notice each segment of you [] is disconnected [] and bolted abruptly
in place [] you have either been dismembered [] or
are about to be.

Each foot [] lower leg [] the thighs [] stomach [] chest [] shoulder
and upper arms [] lower arms [] and these furnace hugging hands
[] they have protection but no dexterity [] there aren't any fingers [] or
the fingers are fused [] it's hard to imagine [] tickling [] stroking
[] hard to imagine juice [] of a woman there glistening.

The most striking thing [] your head [] your body
disconnected [] except for one steel pole [] just open space
between head and all the rest [] and a woman like me
[] curious [] shorter than you [] can stand beneath [] looking up
into where your mind [] could be [] empty except for
pink incursions of light [] in the darkness
of mind [] the cage still round.

The chest too has special reinforcements [] but no heart
to protect [] the heart has abandoned you [] replicated itself
into hundreds of hearts [] all glass [] and screwed [] to the wall
in a row [] some respond to my touch [] my warmth [] a beam
[] a shaft [] of coloured light [] a tension [] attention I crave.

But not you hurt locker [] I get nothing from you [] touching is
forbidden [] I am sure this is your wish [] I walk [] round and
around [] a hexagon of black tape [] marks the floor [] makes me
keep [] this distance.

I walk round and around [] you never walk around me [] I can't
even get [] the light to play [] on you.

But sometimes [] on your back [] when we are not facing each other
[] I see shards of orange [] it gives me something [] if I move
my head [] I can make them touch [] merge [] divide [] cells
at play [] in some stilted way [] an interaction.

To be honest I get the most joy [] when I peer through the spaces
where your segments are separated [] your very dismembering allows
relief [] from relentless steel squares [] space allows the light to get in []
to get out [] to glint [] the colour of confidence [] so they say.

And there [] a triumph [] if I come [] too close [] to where
I am forbidden if I cross [] that black line I see [] my little heads
[] reflected in three of your squares [] one on
top of the other [] a vertical arrangement.

This seems to satisfy me [] at last this glimpse [] of myself [] my multiplication [] three squares [] like screens under one [] of your arms [] enough to keep me interested [] to keep me [] peering into every space between your [] segmentation.

I recognise [] at last [] this is love [] each bulge of glass expanding through each [] steel square [] somehow looks like a jewel [] a dark ruby as if [] your inside is now outside [] the jewel bulges [] through every girder [] every inch of scaffold.

I want to pass my hand between your torso [] your head [] where all good necks should be [] waiting for an axe [] that mind-body split always [] aches the size of space [] allows the light [] to infiltrate [] that's what makes you the jewel [] the duel.

Now I know you better [] I am moving myself [] I can almost make every square [] of your body [] light up [] but how many years would I have [] to circumnavigate [] to keep you lit.

If I step back [] to the entrance and turn [] on the beat [] the whistling [] of blood in glass hearts [] you do [] almost [] look lit [] thrumming with electricity as if [] you could walk off [] stiffly of course [] but under your own impulse [] perhaps you are not contingent [] upon me [] to make us shine.

I see a smile [] is it? [] a smirk in the curl [] of steel across your face [] are you smug [] you have made me [] do [] all the work.

I hate to leave you [] you make me [] remember [] the cage I once wore [] the tiny ways [] I started [] to let things in [] and out [] hard at first [] no one wants [] to want [] glass can be broken [] a cage protects [] a cage traps [] but with heat [] look what a cage can create.

one last excursion

when my parents broke up
my father took us on one last
excursion as a family
the royal melbourne show

my mother went on the ferris wheel
even though she hates rides
even though she is scared of heights
moths and wings and unknown things

she wanted to prove she was not
a fraidy cat to show him she was
worthy of love that wheel
it is still going round

shower poem 1987

my mother cleans
her own cage
all day long

she wants us to help her
we want
to dismantle
the whole bloody thing
bar by iron bar
and build
a railway track out of here

naked
but for her gloves
and thongs and shower cap
she screams for us to return

her voice carries

but she won't get ready
to come with us
and we won't
let the bars
become the scaffolding
from which we are lowered
into the earth

my mother stole my father's death

it was brand new
I only had it a week
I avoided visiting her
so I could keep it   that little bit longer

when I pulled up
she threw all his faults and excuses
in my direction before I even
got out of the car

she thought I should catch her words stroke them
like I always did
        after all I've been through she cried
but I had my arms full of his death
it was heavy and awkward to carry

she followed me round
and round the house
me carrying my father's death
and she years of bitterness
        exploding

her words
avalanched around me
blocking the narrow path I had chosen

eventually I had to drop my father's death at her feet
like washing   in a damp tangled pile

and send myself
deep inside
to lie down

she kept circling the house
gripping the ajax   as she always did
talking to herself loudly   as she always did
I couldn't get away

cursing she wiped his reflection off the bench
in furious circling motions
all afternoon

at dusk she collapsed into a chair   triumphant!
he belonged to her at last
and so did I

unfinished

after Mirka Mora
ink drawing and watercolour on paper scroll, unfinished

Ω

the smell of paint and wood
and dust and pleasure as I open the box
as I gently unroll it just keeps going
an empty white wondering of
what next a slide into living creatures
everybody leaning forward from their outlines
from darkened gaps
then a lavish flush
a camaraderie of colour

Ω

the creatures are snuggled together
though completely and quietly distinct

there are chickens birds crocodiles and dogs
pigs geese and mermaids the people with wings
the people without wings some naked some clothed
half human half animal a cockatoo and some
with flowers growing out of opened-up heads

they are woven with pinks yellows reds
softened with green mauve and blue
I feel delight in the colours most of all
a harmony the warmth of human
affection a complementarity
not one colour dominates

or shouts or forces another one out
and none hide or fade

the creatures are pressed together
in this scrolling unfinished story
each touching but not holding too tightly
not trying to change the others
or set them in human state
stop the drift into animal

there are ducks with human bodies
persons partly human partly fish
all this strange togetherness
bodies leaning casually or sprawling
loose as if they'd just been loved in a climate
with never a need for covers

towards the middle an older woman with wings
a broad face not yet fully coloured
could it be mirka an angel?

on her right every creature is painted
strange sentient beings united by colour

on her left black on white outlines
of characters waiting for their colour
which is not now coming

mirka you did not try to save
a single one of these creatures
you just admired them fondly
you have seen them exactly as they are
invited them to belong on your long scroll
all shapes and wild ages and natures
and between them an excess of wing

Ω

I wonder why I can't commingle
with all my people instead of trying
to change them make them happier
why can't I rejoice in their spirit and
allow them their quirks their
patch on this grand unfurling scroll
that will not go on
forever?

Ω

a little girl beside a mother unhappy
a sister unhappy how she tried
to make them happy
how she failed and she failed
she tried harder held tighter
controlled more of their lives
she believed if she tried
she could make them all closer
to normal

Ω

mirka the mural of my life is not as you rendered
a gargantuan gargoyle sits smack in the middle
a happy machine a self-improvement machine
it dominates the mural people huddle round edges
afraid of its mouth like they were of the trains
come to take them away no one in colour
I drained it all out

a big spout on the left to push people in
and a spout on the right to spit them back out
as new improved versions more cheerful more normal
how is it my job to feed
and maintain the machine?

I feed them all in and they never come out
any different any happier
I am failing I am failing
so I feed myself in and I run
back around dive into the spout
this is my orbit I never seem to improve
or turn out more happy just hierarchy
a kind of control
that impersonates helping
my straining and failing
exhausting

Ω

I didn't settle in any of the murals I saw
now I find myself alone
with a self-portrait oh mirka

can I nestle in here beside you? become
one of your creatures will you web-up my feet
and wing both my blades
a beak will be fine as long as it can smile
I would like some colour a blush or a peach
or the pink of a melon but please mirka white over
my misery machine in the space add more
people maybe mermaids I don't care
if I am never quite finished
it's a relief being left
with some of my lines
undone

loving the eliza way

i running

when you see something
you love you run towards it
and I run after you
something I love

ii wet shoes

splish splash left right
splish splash hold hands
as we stomp in the puddles
you jump right in
to the very thing the
adults try to avoid

iii over-tired

you crawl through the tables
and chairs and the chatter
every time I try to pick you
up you yell ow ow owie
and everyone thinks
I am hurting you badly
and I think of all the times
in my life I was tired
and frustrated and wanted to
to scream ow ow owie
and force someone else
to give up to give in
to give me my own way

iv wriggling

you are on the couch
beside me and instead
of wriggling to get away
you wriggle in closer
you pick up my arm
and wrap it around you
like a blanket you tuck it in
and then we are still

tiger power

eliza eliza eliza jane
if you were a tiger
you wouldn't be tame
you'd be wild and ferocious
and full of life
you wouldn't have skin
you'd be covered in stripes
you'd be orange and black
and you'd run from your cave
you would help all the cubs
and be terribly brave
I would pat you and love you
and be very proud
and wonder how
your roar got so loud
I know you're not really
a tiger at all
but a sweet little girl
who is five and not four!
but you carry the heart
of the tiger in you
it will help you be strong
when you need it to
whisper 'tiger oh tiger'
under your breath
the big tiger spirit
will do all the rest
happy birthday eliza
wow you are five!
I have never met a girl
(or a tiger) so fully alive
I love you
every single hour
I'm ever so glad you have
tiger power

ferocious moon

after Shams of Tabriz

I
don't suppose
I can stay like this
forever? seeing everything
hearing everything being touched
by everything in that one invisible place
I ache for the beginning the ending which I know
are the same I wait weaving bed clothes by night
unravelling the thread each day when my yearning becomes
unbearable shams reminds me don't forget the moon! my skin
glowing under its gaze my shadow barely following my once dead
body as I float through white teeth light I know full well that in
days to come god will pare off the edge soften the moon to
a dint a crooked smile a barely luminous crack in the dark until
nothing but black everything taken from me but I hear shams
whisper roll over look up! stars are raining down in the
sky in the once dark pit of your stomach the moon will
grow back shams insists it will frighten you again
roar at you with ferocious light meanwhile
unbutton your shirt right down to the
waist stars are trying to get your
attention they want to
pierce your
skin

moon grief

I have started to grieve
thirty-seven-year-old eve
she was full and round
and emitted mysterious light
but she contracted and became
          over time
              a bit flattened on one side
                  then a half
                    a sliver
                          a hairline crack

oh the thick black absence
that stretched across my face
yes for a time in the dark
there was no such eve

but out in the night
thirty-eight-year-old eve
against all odds
began to be born
a cut of light at first
she thickened and
swelled
almost full

a crown
between knees
of mountains

circles on water

for Robyn Frances

i mounds

easter after easter someone is killed
and someone crawls out of a cave

hair is cut it lays dormant by the verandah
until the pile is carried into forest on open hands
as if it were nest it will become nest another nest
overnight a web was stretched between every desolate
tree now wrapped in a shawl of jewels or drips
or tears a choir of trees and I notice the relationship
between each piece of wood living and dead
upright or piled or packed under tin or just leaning
into each other

there are circles inside every wooden body
stacked here on earth parts that touch
and crevices between where nothing but
little living legs scuttle the rhythm of looking
for safety and sun safety and sun
waiting for cold blood to be warmed

ii reflection

a shared pool to look into where palm trees
are reflected and turned upside down see the
frayed fronds the oldest and driest browning
their way to death yes I see it myself: a height
that grows down as much as it grows up a stingray
of cloud a billowing patience in the watery below

iii muscle

there is practise between us the verb not
the noun this practise on pages with poems
or with paint you are making pink hearts to hang
in the ear of a stranger they are held in your hands
they are punctured by dremel it is the practise
of making though it might be the practise
of staying alive

it is a parallel play this pushing of world
like the cat pushes you when you're trying
to sleep paw against arm nail in or nail ouch
we will forgive this resistance we both nestle
and strain on our leads yes we want and don't
want to be tethered

iv raspberries

I bring you raspberries floating in clear water
I notice the 'p' and I notice the drupelets
tiny spheres that somehow stick together
each one a loose heart bobbing amongst bubbles
that is what I learn in your presence to bob
up and down with all of my colour
let myself gradually turn all the waters
around me a softer pink and you bring me some
blueberries bobbing in their own hissing drink
and it turns the colour of bruise with its own
kind of beauty a reminder to be tender

v larger

even in water so still all the circles grow larger grow
outwards there is not one ring
that contracts

vi floating

I look at you now and am happy to see
that you float and I float there is nothing wrong
with our devices

the dragonflies cross over our water
in no single direction
when they pause on our leaves or our books
we look closely
their red tails throbbing

the fern I am

see the fern I am
trying to describe I am
wondering if it has teeth or is more
like feather like fringe
a bat flies through an opening
and I wonder if I should mention
how its poo corrodes the paint
on my car or just say simply
that it must fall from a tree
in order to gain the momentum
to fly and that's why
it hangs there upside down
trying to sleep but all ready to go
that creeper a weed a climber
or is it a beautiful connection
between water in a jar and
the air the warmth and what about that
jar is it prison or container or a
marvellous transparency an opportunity
to see roots growing and coiling
without the opaqueness of soil
and the phone calling just now is it
interruption intrusion or another
opportunity to love to root
like the creeper connecting the water
within and the sky above tubers
you tie us to earth although
we are ringed in vessel
and spend all our days climbing

the cubans understand

I stretch out on the couch
away from the heat but it is everywhere

your hands guide my head
onto your pregnant lap

you pluck my grey hairs out laughing
one by laughing one

I protest then well with delight
that a single thread of hair connects us

you teach me the spanish word for grey hair it is different
from grey eyes grey clouds

you pluck away each pallid thread as if the truth
around each root could not surprise you and I am released

to wander along your gentle brown hair
parting like a river over bare shoulders

the heat has joined us for today
there is no water to scoop over ourselves in tinfuls

to wash ourselves
separate

your husband enters the room
like one long smile

he takes a photograph of your belly
your baby with you and I grinning behind her

I wish she could curl her little fingers
round our friendship but by then

I will be gone

on the back of your bike

I'm leaning into you
you want me to sit up straight

I try to draw the warmth out of you
like I do when I lie behind you in bed

you tell me
not to lean

my spine stiffens in offence
I am repelled backwards

off the end of the bike
through time and space to

another place where
I was left sitting on the ground

mouth open while a man
drove away from me

Ω

you stop the bike for a moment
I hop off stumbling

in the suit you loaned me
thick as old tyres

I'm sure I put something of myself
into one of these pockets

but as I pat myself down
I can no longer feel the shape

of my own body or anything solid
that once belonged to me

I get back on the bike but by now
we have perfected a wall between us

Ω

at home the wall surrounds you
like a circumference

I try to put myself
in your line of vision

you look behind me or in front
I have lent too far towards you

you will not get close enough
for it to happen again

once you cured my shivering
with the heat of your body

now I am left to generate my own heat
and I realise I cannot make enough

in this iron shed we call home
lined with boards nailed next to each other

way too soon that have shrunk and recoiled
leaving silver-foiled disappointment

Ω

an unlit fire no source of heat
except my own body

I curl into it like stone you have gone
to the forest taking the dog for warmth

I am left with a fur-coated blanket
but none of the fur is attached

I crouch in the abandoned fireplace
a stone amongst stones

screwing up paper furiously
and throwing it into a pile

as if each sheet was my birth certificate
and needed to be destroyed

there is one solitary match in the box
and I am afraid to strike it

it's not until I watch you ride away
on your bike for good

leaning into the curve of the road
that I even have the courage to try

storm music

you are trapped inside a grand body | it is the world
but it feels like a womb | or it is a womb that feels
like the world | it is dark | you are nothing but absence
| you are warm | everything is warm | there is a flash
of light a flickering | you think of mary shelley | you
think of the absent bolts in your absent neck

there is a low growling now | it is coming
towards you | you wonder what will happen when you
finally meet it | water is battering this cage | it grows
louder and harder | you wanted the water to fill you
but you are no longer a vessel | you are no longer
anything that matters

frogs sing like the springs
on a mattress that someone is jumping on | and on | and
on |

she of the grand body picks up her cello | she
places it between open knees | she picks up a bow |
you have become a carapace | and you get a strange
new sense | something inside you is worth protecting |
persevering with

it's only when she starts to play
that you realise you are not an absence | you are five
thick strings stretched | and she pulls at you |
you make sound | at first just a groaning | of surprise
really | that you can feel

yes there are things inside
you | and she | has made them move

venus

I dine alone
a rock for my table
for my chair
the beach my new bar
drinking red wine
from a pesto jar
my salad in a box
the other people
at this restaurant
are all couples
it's like dining
on valentine's day
one star so bright
it shines like a cross
the new venus

afterword

between each eclipse

some days the door behind you closes
and you look through the foliage for an opening
you are prepared to shrink and squeeze

through the narrowest entrance knowing
that smaller worlds might well be
the most interesting and it is pleasing

for you not to be one more awkward giant
that crushes and bumps into everything
causing great calamity you can pass through

you can move aside a branch without bruising
leaves or battering flower from stem there are
insects like this that hover over water

long bodies throbbing red to be so close
to something that alive without disturbing it
without the hammer and anvil and heat

without forcing it into an arch to be nailed
to a hoof as beautiful as iron also is
things fall here one by one they drift and on

gentle descent catch light in each intricate
edge of their being these airborne dancers
the petal the seed the carcass of insect

dislodged from a tiny platform where it took
shelter there is a cell of light on my wall
bouncing like ball and then stretching apart

each half moving in opposite directions as if
it is about to become two of whatever it once was
I suppose this is the beginning this invisible pull

before separation the purpose is cryptic it cannot
be to descend as no sooner has something
landed and been crushed underfoot it grows

wet and disintegrates into the soil that it was
then ascending again through some green straw
to become leaf that too will be lost but nor can

the purpose be to ascend for only bats to enjoy
and send scattering down tattered leaves or
smattered shit which has it uses even on days

like today we remember there are explosives
and cyclones and expositions when almost
everything will be torn from that which it was

happily holding on to these moments of drift
between disaster when we are loosened from
striving and reaching are worth watching

notice it is raining blossom and the leaves
overhead keep shaping and reshaping the sun
on the deck a lazy expansion between each eclipse

Acknowledgements

This book was written in many locations from Dover to Darwin, and in many different homes for which I am grateful. Thanks to Sue and Karen for the life-changing Cape Paterson and for Daylesford and your friendship and faith in my work; Jenny Gee and Pete for Patersonia and Mags and pademelons, and for being here with me before; Melissa and Joanna for Eastside and sitting beside me as I lay on the floor; Jane Ulrik for home, beer and tea under your tree; Bec, Liz and Eliza for pillow fights and the way you welcome me every single time; Lorraine and Lockie for my childhood home in Maryborough; Lorraine for being the mother I rubbed up against all these years trying to carve myself out; Julie and Annabelle and the love always at Carisbrook; Linda, Joe and Matilda and the love always at West Melbourne; Colly for dear Williamstown; Beck for Sadadeen and letting me steal your lines; Nina for your home full of treasure and for being a treasure; Amelia for your hands and your steadfastness; Lisa for music and the depth of thought; Kerry for her care and for asking me to photograph everything that was red; Cara for asking the right question; Adrienne for coming to visit me everywhere; Anton for teaching me to light fire in the rain; Corinne for the first Keating note; Caroline and Beth for the reminder about choosing your own ending; Robyn and Ruth for our nest in Nightcliff; Robyn for Edith Piaf and art and poetry and air flowing freely; Michael, Matthew, Michaela, Sally and Luc for *fambly*; Amelia, Sylvia, Sharon, Tish and all the Arrernte women from Akeyulerre who wrote *Arelhekenhe Angkentye: Women's Talk—lyapirtneme* was my return too; Dani Powell for lyapirtneme, festivals and friendship; Penny Byrne for North Fitzroy, Hurt Locker, Mirka's Box and the Fennec Fox; Deb for operculum and Heather for speaking truths; Paul Collis for Blackie; Jenny Taylor for helping me see myself again and Sue Fielding for shelter; Ilan for his departure poem and its refrain; Craig San Roque for his uncanny Jungian companionship over ten years; To the many people who showed me kindness on a difficult journey; Shari Kocher for poetic prowess and close reading; Johanna Bell and Peter Bakowski for different kinds of encouragement; Mary Anne Butler for the glass doors to what's next; Kirby for jumping up on me. And dear Fran, thanks to you, for all we have been through together and apart. You left some of yourself nestled inside me, and I hope I left something worthwhile nestled in you.

Special thanks to Jordie Albiston for her skill and touch in editing the manuscript, her wisdom in ordering the poems, and her juxtaposition of poetic phrases to create the section titles. The drawings that open each section were created by Robyn Frances in response to these titles. I cannot sufficiently express my gratitude for these gifts. *I am the glass* is enriched by Jordie and Robyn's 'way of seeing.' I continue to find new perspectives through their contributions. The images are: (1) A moon made of endings; (2) A binary star system—two stars gravitationally bound to each other; (3) A sea eagle nest, which also appears on the cover. I thank Recent Work Press for the cover design.

Thanks to Shane Strange from Recent Work Press for his insight, support and stewardship. He made the work stronger, and let me be stubborn on occasion, it is always a pleasure working alongside him. Any failings in the book are mine alone.

'nightcliff' was a finalist in Northern Territory Literary Awards Poetry Prize in 2019 and first appeared in the anthology of finalists.

'darwin (a prelude)' first appeared in the *Australian Poetry Anthology* Volume 7, 2019.

'fallen' was a finalist in the NT Literary Awards Poetry Prize in 2011 and first appeared in the anthologies of finalists.

I wish to acknowledge the art works that gave rise to the ekphrastic poems:

'hurt locker'

Penny Byrne (b. 1965)
Hurt Locker, 2015
Blown glass, steel
Hurt Locker stands, as a suit of armour, over two metres in height created for the Venice Biennale. It was later exhibited at the Canberra Glassworks, in the 'Hearts and Minds' Exhibition, 2018. This exhibition included a corridor of extraordinary glass hearts created by Harriet Schwarzrock that responded to touch. 'Hearts and Minds' was curated by Jane Cush.

'horse and swallow'

Bronze Galloping Horse Treading on a Flying Swallow, a statue situated near Lake Burleigh Griffin, Canberra.

The plaque reads: 'Regarded as a national treasure this is a famous representative sculpture is from the Eastern Han Dynasty (25-220 AD). The original sculpture was unearthed in Wuwei County, Gansu Province. This reproduction depicts the Heavenly Stead of Chinese Legend, in dynamic flight with one hoof stepping on the back of a swallow, accentuating the speed and power of the horse.'

'unfinished'

Mirka Mora (1928—2018)
Untitled, unfinished
Ink drawing and watercolour on paper scroll from the private collection of Penny Byrne, viewed in December 2019.

'song for a weary throat'

Song for a Weary Throat
Theatre production
Devised and performed by RAWCUS Ensemble, Theatre Works, St Kilda, December 2017.
Directed by Kate Sulan. The three singers were Gian Slater, Josh Kyle and Louisa Ranki
The words in italics are quotes from the performance.

'portrait'

Eliza Jane Dowty-Drysdale (b. 2015)
This is Penny, 2017
Texta drawing on paper

'thirty million steps'

This is a found poem and the words belong to artist Marina Abramović, as published in *Getting There: A Book of Mentors*, edited by Gillian Zoe Segal, 2015.

Thirty million steps is the number of steps estimated to comprise the Great Wall of China.

The epigraph by Patrizia Cavalli was translated from Italian by Mark Strand with Gini Alhadeff, and appeared in the book *Patrizia Cavalli, My Poems Won't Change the World.*

The epigraph by Mary Oliver, is an excerpt from the poem 'Franz Marc's Blue Horses' and appeared in Mary Oliver's book, *Blue Horses.*

The poem **'the cubans understand'** references a love poem by Peter Bakowski, 'The Spanish Understand'.

About the Author

Penny Drysdale grew up in central Victoria and lived in Alice Springs for seven years working at the Arrernte-run Akeyulerre Healing Centre. She is currently a lawyer and policy adviser in Darwin conducting projects to reduce domestic violence. Penny won the NT Literary Awards Poetry Prize in 2015 and her first book of poetry *Dew and Broken Glass* was published by Recent Work Press in 2017. Penny is editor of a book of poetry written by Arrernte women in Central Australia called *Arelhekenhe Angkentye: Women's Talk* on the theme of *Lyapirtneme* | *Return* (Ptilotus Press, 2020). *I am the glass* is her second book of poetry.

Lightning Source UK Ltd.
Milton Keynes UK
UKHW011003040521
383105UK00001B/60

9 780645 009026